A Short-Term **DISCIPLE** Bible Study

INVITATION
OLD TESTAMENT
TO THE

LEADER GUIDE

D0406301

Abingdon Press
Nashville

A Short-Term DISCIPLE Bible Study

INVITATION TO THE OLD TESTAMENT

LEADER GUIDE

Copyright © 2005 by Abingdon Press
All rights reserved

Harriett Jane Olson, Senior Vice President of Publishing and Editor of Church School Publications; Mark Price, Senior Editor; Cindy Caldwell, Development Editor; Kent Sneed, Design Manager; Leo Ferguson, Designer

10 11 12 13 14 — 10 9 8 7 6 5 4 3 2

Contents

Introducing
This Study Series

INVITATION TO THE OLD TESTAMENT is one of a series of studies developed on the model of DISCIPLE Bible study. DISCIPLE is a family of Bible study resources based on the general assumption that people are hungry for God's Word, for fellowship in prayer and study, and for biblically informed guidance in ministry. This series of Short-Term DISCIPLE Bible Studies, like all long-term DISCIPLE resources, (1) presents the Bible as the primary text, (2) calls for daily preparation on the part of students, (3) features a weekly meeting based on small group discussion, (4) includes a video component for making available the insights of biblical scholars to set the Scriptures in context, and (5) has as one of its goals the enhancement of Christian discipleship.

INVITATION TO THE OLD TESTAMENT is designed to provide congregations with an in-depth, high-commitment Bible study resource able to be completed in a shorter time frame than the foundational DISCIPLE studies. The shorter time frame, however, does not mean this study has expectations different from those associated with the thirty-four week DISCIPLE: BECOMING DISCIPLES THROUGH BIBLE STUDY. The expectation remains that participants will prepare for the weekly meeting by reading substantial portions of Scripture and taking notes. The expectation remains that group discussion, rather than lecture, will be the preferred learning approach. The expectation remains that biblical scholarship will be part of the group's study together. The expectation remains that persons' encounter with the Bible will call them to more faithful discipleship. Hopefully, in fact, one of the chief benefits of studies in the Short-Term DISCIPLE Bible Study series, will be how well they inspire persons to commit to a long-term DISCIPLE study in the future. For, while these short studies of selected Scriptures can be both meaningful and convenient, the deeply transforming experience of reading and studying all the Scriptures, from Genesis to Revelation, continues to be the primary aim of DISCIPLE.

Leading This Study

For leaders of INVITATION TO THE OLD TESTAMENT, it will be vital to keep in mind that, to have as rich and meaningful a study experience as possible with this type of short-term study, you will need to pay close attention to the timing of the suggested discussion activities and group dynamics. One of the challenges of any short-term, small-group study—especially one based on group discussion—is the time it takes for people in the study to become comfortable sharing with one another. If your group is made up of people who are already acquainted, the challenge may be minimal. However, be prepared to have a group of people who do not know each other well, perhaps some who have never done much substantive Bible study, others who are graduates of long-term DISCIPLE studies. Make use of the following information as you prepare to lead INVITATION TO THE OLD TESTAMENT.

GROUP ORIENTATION

Plan to schedule an orientation meeting a week prior to the first weekly meeting. Take time then to make introductions, discuss the expectations of the study, distribute and review the materials, and preview the upcoming week's assignment. Be sure to alert group members to the "Digging Deeper" boxes that appear after the commentary sections. If necessary, consider discussing the kind of study Bible group members should use and taking time to be sure everyone is familiar with the aids in a study Bible. Have on hand several types of study Bibles for persons to look through.

THE WEEKLY SESSION

The times in parentheses, beneath each section heading in the leader guide planning pages, indicate the suggested numbers of minutes to allow for a particular activity. The first time is for use with a 60-minute meeting schedule and the second time is for use with a 90-minute meeting. Keep in mind that it is always possible the discussion questions suggested for use in any one section will be more than enough to take up the allotted time. The leader will need to keep an eye on a clock and decide when and whether to move on. The best way to gauge, in advance, how many questions to use and how long to allow discussion to last is to spend time answering the suggested questions while preparing for the group session. Be sure to do that, as well as preview the video, both Part 1 and Part 2, before the weekly session.

Gathering Around God's Word

(15–20 minutes)

Welcome

Begin on time by welcoming the group to the study. Ideally, this should be the *second* time the group has been together. During the orientation meeting the previous week, group participants met to preview the materials, discuss expectations of the study, and receive the assignment for the week. In case group participants arrive at this first session who were not present at the orientation meeting, be prepared to summarize as briefly as possible what they can expect from the study and what the study will expect from them.

Invitation to the Table (Optional)

In keeping with the theme of invitation, each week, consider setting up a small table somewhere in the meeting room. The table will serve as a focal point for the group. The suggestions in this section include a list of items to consider placing on the table and a question. While the items placed on the table require no discussion, the question is intended for reflection and brief discussion. Both the question and the table items are designed to connect a central theme of the week's study with the participants' own experience. While this is an option for the group, it may well serve to establish a sense of community within the group.

Prayer

Establish a particular ritual of praying together at the start of the study. Keep in mind that the text of this study, the Bible, is a rich source of meaningful prayers. When appropriate, make use of other Bible translations when praying the Scriptures. A suggested portion from a Psalm will appear in this section each week; that same Psalm text also appears in the "Daily Assignments" section of the participant book for use as daily prayer. Be sure to include group members in this process by inviting willing participants to lead in prayer.

Invitation From Scripture

At the close of the prayer time and just before introducing the first video segment, a theme verse is to be read aloud. This reading is intended as an invitation to the session, serving to invite or invoke God's presence, and to give voice to the theme of the week's study. The first question in the "For Reflection" section in each session's commentary in the participant book will call attention to this text. Each week, ask a different participant to read the passage for the group or have the group read it in unison, just before introducing the first video segment.

Viewing the Video: Session 1, Part 1

The video component in the series has two parts and both parts are central to the group's study. Part 1 is a ten-minute presentation by a biblical scholar on some topic related to the Scriptures and themes in the week's readings. The purpose of this video is to provide a common base of additional information about or interpretation of the Scriptures for the group to discuss. A brief summary of this video appears in the leader guide plan for each session.

Encountering God's Word in the Text

(20–25 minutes)

In this section, group discussion centers on some of the Scripture passages read during the week.

Examining God's Word in Context

(15–20 minutes)

Viewing the Video: Session 1, Part 2

The focus in this section is on viewing Part 2 of the video. This video features an informal, unscripted presentation by a biblical scholar. Like

Part 1, this presentation pertains to some theme that emerges from the week's readings or to some of the texts themselves and is designed to prompt further discussion. **Note:** An intentional characteristic of Part 2 is its informality. As a result, on occasion the presenter may stumble over a word or jumble a phrase. Be aware of that. Sometimes retaining the flow of the presentation was more advisable than trying to excise a verbal miscue.

The information in this video segment is designed to illuminate the biblical texts by the light of recent archaeological evidence. The presentation, on its own, may prompt sufficient discussion by the group. In other words, simply following up the video with questions such as "What photograph or insight caught your attention?" or "How does this information inform our readings for this week?" may be enough to start and sustain a discussion. In addition, the instructions in this section suggest three other approaches for use in following up the video segment. Often, one or more of these approaches assumes that group participants will come to the weekly session having done extra reading or research in a Bible dictionary or Bible atlas as part of their preparation. When previewing the upcoming week's assignment, always alert the group to the "Digging Deeper" box printed at the end of each session's commentary in the participant book. Also, have on hand several copies (print versions) of Bible dictionaries or Bible atlases for the group to use. A brief list of recommended Bible reference resources (including some electronic editions) appears in the participant book on page 10. Having as many of these resources available for group participants to use will enhance their study and enrich their discussion following Part 2 of the video.

Going Forth With God's Word: An Invitation to Discipleship

(10–15 minutes)

Consideration of the implications of the week's readings on the call of Christian discipleship is the point of this section. The discussion questions in the leader guide plan for each session come from questions raised in the commentary and the "For Reflection" sections of the participant book. Be alert to additional questions that come to mind and might be useful at this time in the group meeting.

Closing and Prayer

Turn to the next session and preview the lesson and the assignments for the week ahead. Establish a pattern of inviting prayer concerns and praying together at this time.

GROUP DYNAMICS

The effectiveness of the group's study together depends heavily upon the way you, as the leader, manage individual participation. Plan for the majority of the weekly discussion to take place in smaller groups of three or four or in pairs. Smaller groupings will give everyone more opportunity to talk and is the best way for people to get to know one another quickly. Smaller groupings will reduce the possibility that a couple of people will dominate the conversation or that some will not contribute at all. Smaller groupings communicate that preparation is expected and essential for fruitful discussion.

Also key to the effectiveness of the group's study together is how you manage your role as the leader. Remember: your primary role is to facilitate the process, not to provide the information. To that end, follow these basic guidelines as you lead the study:

- Prepare exactly as participants prepare; see yourself as a learner among learners.
- Know where the discussion is heading from the outset; this will minimize the chances of getting sidetracked along the way.
- Set ground rules for group participation and maintenance early on; doing so will encourage the whole group to take responsibility for monitoring itself.
- Be a good listener; don't be afraid of silence—allow time for people to think before responding.

The Making of the Hebrew Bible

Gathering Around God's Word

(15–20 minutes)

Welcome

Begin on time by welcoming the group to the study. Ideally, this should be the *second* time the group has been together. During the orientation meeting the previous week, group participants met to preview the materials, discuss expectations of the study, and receive the assignment for the week. In case group participants arrive at this first session who were not present at the orientation meeting, be prepared to summarize as briefly as possible what they can expect from the study and what the study will expect from them.

Invitation to the Table (Optional)

In keeping with the theme of invitation, each week set up a small table somewhere in the meeting room. The table will serve as a thematic focal point for the group. The suggestions in this section include a list of items to place on the table and an opening question for reflection and brief discussion. Both the question and the table items are designed to connect the themes of the week's readings with the participants' own experience.

- **Opening question:** What Bible story do you remember hearing as a child, and how was it told to you?
- **Items for the table:** seashell; flower; picture of a rainbow; picture of family; list of rules; law books; ashes; cooking pot; branch; an old, worn map.

Prayer
- Psalm 119:105-112

Read together

Establish a particular ritual of praying together at the start of the study. Keep in mind that the text of this study, the Bible, is a rich source of meaningful prayers. When appropriate, make use of other Bible translations when praying the Scriptures. A suggested portion of a passage from a Psalm will appear in this section each week; that same Psalm text also appears in the "Daily Assignments" section of the participant book for use as a daily prayer. Be sure to include group members in this process by inviting those participants who are willing to lead in prayer.

Invitation From Scripture

Assemble the people for me, and I will let them hear my words, so that they may learn to fear me as long as they live on earth, and may teach their children so. —Deuteronomy 4:10

The passage printed here is intended to be read aloud as an invitation to the weekly session, serving to invite or invoke God's presence and to give voice to the theme of the week's study. One of the questions for reflection and discussion by the group at the end of the session will call attention to this verse. Each week, ask a different participant to read it for the group, or have the group read it in unison, just before introducing the first video segment.

Viewing the Video: Session 1, Part 1

(Also, view **Introduction** if not shown during an orientation meeting.)

Prepare to View Video:

Listen for the three parts of the Hebrew canon. Note the metaphor of a map and how this metaphor is used in describing the Old Testament.

Summary of Video Content:

Canon means "standard" or "measurement." It refers to the list of authorized texts we consider as sacred Scriptures. The community of faith formed the biblical canon over a long period of time. If the canon were viewed as a map and we could look back through the layers, we would see centuries of development and change based on the community's usage and needs.

The Hebrew Bible became Holy Scripture in three stages, which corresponds to its three parts. The Law or Torah (the first five books of the Bible), represents the town center of our map. The Prophets, or Nevi'im, includes the narrative of Israel's history from Joshua through Kings. The Kethuvim, or Writings, represents the paths widening into roads that spanned the length and breadth of the town.

The closing of the canon is usually associated with the Council of Jamnia. Some books were not included. These books were considered interesting side roads rather than texts that were central to the history of Israel.

Like generations before us, we must travel the same roads that have been trod for centuries. We must find our own way in faith using this map we call the Old Testament.

Discuss After Viewing Video:

What story within the Torah would you consider Main Street on the metaphorical map of the Old Testament? On this map, what stories would you consider to be major roads leading from the town center? What major landmarks do you find within the city limits?

Encountering God's Word in the Text

(20–25 minutes)

The readings this week represent some of the voices that are heard in the Bible and the claims these voices make on our lives on behalf of God. Form groups of three or four to examine the variety of voices found in the readings. Instruct each group to work through the Scripture readings for Days 1–5 in this manner: First, talk briefly about what characterizes the voice in that section of Scripture. Then, discuss these questions: What does each voice have to say about God? About God's people? About the relationship between God and God's people?

Choose one of the following passages to read aloud and talk about in the total group:

Genesis 3. The temptation story in Genesis is a story of origins, called an "etiology." Why was knowing how something came to be such an important aspect of the faith traditions of ancient Israel? How do those stories inform our faith today?

Jeremiah 1:1–2:3. What is the reward and the challenge of being the mouthpiece for God? When have you found yourself in the role of having to speak a word on behalf of God? What was the response of those who heard the message?

Examining God's Word in Context

(15–20 minutes)

The Old Testament or Hebrew Bible took on its current form over a long period of time. New archaeological finds and centuries of interpretation enable us to better understand God's covenantal love for us and God's call on our lives.

Viewing the Video: Session 1, Part 2

Prepare to View Video:
Listen for the archaeological discoveries that have made an impact on the Old Testament or Hebrew Bible.

Discuss After Viewing Video:
The information in this video segment is designed to illuminate the biblical texts by the light of recent archaeological evidence. The presentation, on its own, may prompt sufficient discussion by the group. In other words, simply following up the video with questions such as "What photograph or insight caught your attention?" or "How does this information inform our readings for this week?" may be enough to start and sustain a discussion. In addition, the instructions in this section suggest three other approaches for use in following up the video segment. Often, one or more of these approaches assumes that group participants will come to the weekly session having done extra reading or research in a Bible dictionary or Bible atlas as part of their preparation. When previewing the upcoming week's assignment, always alert the group to the "Digging Deeper" box printed at the end of the commentary in the participant book. Also, have on hand several copies (print versions) of Bible dictionaries or Bible atlases for the group to use. A brief list of recommended Bible reference resources (including some electronic editions) appears in the participant book on page 10.

After Viewing Video:
While the presentation, on its own, may prompt sufficient discussion by the group, consider one or more of the following approaches to guide the group's response to the information in the video segment.

❖ **Making Connections:** How does knowing that the text of the Old Testament was carefully copied and passed down faithfully for seventeen hundred years affect how we read that text today?

❖ **Digging Deeper:** Hear what group members learned from reading articles about or descriptions of the following items in a Bible dictionary: Dead Sea Scrolls, Septuagint, and Masoretic text. Talk about what those textual sources contribute to the Bible we use today.

❖ **Looking Further:** Have available a copy of a TANAKH translation of the Hebrew Bible, with the Hebrew text and English translation (published by the Jewish Publication Society); or a copy of the *Biblia Hebraica Stuttgartensia*; or an interlinear Hebrew-English Old Testament. Pass it around for the group to view the Hebrew characters, the dots and dashes, known as "the pointing system" (cantillation), and the order of the books. Using various translations, examine the Scriptures mentioned in the video segment: Isaiah 53:11; 1 Samuel 11; Psalm 22:16.

Going Forth With God's Word: An Invitation to Discipleship

(10–15 minutes)

Centuries in the making, the Hebrew Bible is part of our Scriptures today. How we approach the Old Testament will determine what we gain from it.

In pairs, discuss the following questions:
- What has been your approach to reading the Old Testament?
- What stories or events from the Old Testament speak with relevance to you today?
- What keeps you from listening attentively to the various voices in the Old Testament so that you accurately hear what God is saying?

Conclude discussion by calling attention to the "For Reflection" section on page 25 in the participant book. Ask pairs to share responses to one or more of the questions in that section.

Closing and Prayer

Turn to Session 2 and preview the focus of the lesson and the assignments for the week ahead. Be sure to alert group members to the information in the "Digging Deeper" box on page 37 of the participant book. Establish a pattern of inviting prayer concerns and praying together at this time.

The Creation Story of Israel

Gathering Around God's Word

(15–20 minutes)

Welcome
Begin on time by welcoming the group to the study.

Invitation to the Table (Optional)
- **Opening question:** What was your parent's faith and how did that influence you?
- **Items for the table:** snapshots of family members, a wedding album, pictures of desert regions (Sinai Peninsula, Egypt, Mesopotamia), sand

Prayer
✳ • Psalm 105:1-11 *Read together.*

Invitation From Scripture
✳ *I will bless those who bless you and the one who curses you I will curse; and in you all the families of the earth shall be blessed.* —Genesis 12:3

Viewing the Video: Session 2, Part 1

Prepare to View Video:
Listen for the links and the differences that Judaism, Christianity, and Islam have as descendants of Abraham.

Summary of Video Content:
We tend to identify our religion by what we believe rather than by the families from which we have come. The covenant that God makes with

Abraham in Genesis 12 links both family and religion. What happens to Abraham's family happens to God's promise.

Today, three major world religions stand upon that fusion of family and religion. Judaism, Christianity, and Islam all trace themselves back to Abraham and lay claim to the promise God made to him and his family. These three faith traditions claim ancestry from Abraham for different reasons and for different ends. The legacy of Father Abraham calls some to the practices of Judaism, to circumcision and Torah observance; it calls others to the practices of Christianity and steadfast belief in Jesus; and it calls yet others to the practices of Islam and submission to Allah's (God's) will.

Abraham had to leave the land of his father in order to claim the promises of God. For us to find a world in which all people of the world shall be blessed, we too may need to focus on our future rather than on our past—on what is needed for peace rather than on who can claim Father Abraham.

Discuss After Viewing Video:

How do you respond to the statement, "What happens to Abraham's family happens to God's promise"? Given that Judaism, Christianity, and Islam all share Abraham and all are monotheistic, what accounts for the tensions among these faith families? What does it mean for Christians to claim the promise of God, first made to Abraham?

Encountering God's Word in the Text

(20–25 minutes)

The readings this week are concerned with families. God begins the relationship with the chosen people, Israel, by initiating a covenant with Abraham and Sarah that will be passed down from them to generation after generation. Form three groups to examine the following sets of "covenant encounters" between God and someone:

Group 1: Genesis 12:1-8 and 16:7-16 (Abraham);
Group 2: Genesis 17:1-22, and 21:15-20 (Sarah and Hagar);
Group 3: Genesis 28:10-22 and 32:22-32 (Jacob).

Ask each group to scan the passages to recall the encounters and then to discuss these questions:

- What is the crux of God's covenant promise?
- What does the encounter say about who God is as covenant-maker?
- What does the encounter say about a person's role as covenant-keeper?
- What implications does each "covenant encounter" with God have for other peoples?

As a total group, explore the story of Jacob and Laban in Genesis 29–30. Summarize the conflict and the movements toward reconciliation in the story. Then talk about what the story says about how God's promises work out in the context of family conflict and disunity.

Examining God's Word in Context

(15–20 minutes)

Jews, Christians, and Muslims, two-thirds of the people on the planet, look back to Abraham and call him the father and founder of their faith.

Viewing the Video: Session 2, Part 2

Prepare to View Video:
Listen for information related to Abraham and the archaeological evidence that relates to him.

After Viewing Video:
While the presentation, on its own, may prompt sufficient discussion by the group, consider one or more of the following approaches to guide the group's response to the information in the video segment.

❖ **Making Connections:** Recall the image of the ziggurat in the video. Imagine yourself as Abraham, or as a member of his clan, living in the midst of that civilization, packing up, and moving out across the desert to an unfamiliar land. What kinds of things (possessions, relationships, memories, cultural practices, and so forth) do you leave behind, and what kinds of things do you take with you?

❖ **Digging Deeper:** Dr. Tabor mentions that the word *El*, used in the Bible as part of the name of God, was also used to name the Babylon god. Hear reports from those who looked up the word *El* in a Bible dictionary (*Eerdmans Dictionary of the Bible*, pp. 384–385) or other source (*Understanding the Old Testament*, Anderson, p. 41). How does knowing about the origins and various meanings of *El* inform our understanding of its usage in the story of Abraham?

❖ **Looking Further:** Locate the route Abraham took from Ur "by stages toward the Negeb" on a map in an atlas (*Oxford Bible Atlas*, pp. 54–55) or a study Bible. Try to get a sense of both the distance Abraham traveled and the terrain he encountered. Talk about the significance of Abraham, portrayed as a "wanderer," serving as the focal figure of Israel's story.

Going Forth With God's Word: An Invitation to Discipleship

(10–15 minutes)

The overarching theme of these narratives is the persistence of God's promises in spite of, and on behalf of, God's chosen people. In pairs, discuss the following question: How does a covenant or promise God makes with Abraham thousands of years ago have meaning today? What is our role in helping fulfill God's promise for the world, first given to Abraham?

Conclude discussion by calling attention to the "For Reflection" section on page 36 in the participant book. Ask pairs to share responses to the questions in that section.

Closing and Prayer

Turn to Session 3 and preview the focus of the lesson and the assignments for the week ahead. Be sure to alert group members to the information in the "Digging Deeper" box on page 50 of the participant book.

Out of Bondage

Gathering Around God's Word

(15–20 minutes)

Welcome
Begin on time by welcoming the group to the study.

Invitation to the Table (Optional)
- **Opening question:** If someone asked you to share a moment or event when you sensed God's presence, what would you say?
- **Items for the table:** colorful fabric, bricks, lighted candle, charred branch from a bush, unleavened bread, milk, honey

Prayer
- Psalm 78:12-24

Invitation From Scripture
Even though you intended to do harm to me, God intended it for good, in order to preserve a numerous people, as he is doing today. —Genesis 50:20

Viewing the Video: Session 3, Part 1

Prepare to View Video:
Listen for insights into the story of the Exodus.

Summary of Video Content:
God working in history, determining the outcome of conflicts between people and nations: that image, which runs throughout the Old Testament narrative, is both powerful and ethically complicated. God acts, but humans also make decisions that affect the outcome of events.

It is the power of the Exodus story that is more important than any of its historical details. The story tells about the hopes of the human spirit and the unflagging care of God.

The story of the Exodus offers hope in times of despair, and it suggests that we share with God a responsibility for the outcome of our own history. However God works in history, the choices that humans make also will decide if our future is one of continued suffering or of liberation for all.

Discuss After Viewing Video:
What does the story of the Exodus reveal to us bout God? How is the story of the Exodus part of our story?

Encountering God's Word in the Text

(20–25 minutes)

Journeying from the brick-making fields of Egypt to the wilderness of Sinai, a multitude of Hebrews, delivered by Yahweh and led by Moses, becomes a people called Israel. God acts on behalf of a people to free them from bondage; then God speaks the covenant community into being. In groups of three or four, examine the assigned Scripture readings from Exodus for Days 3, 4, and 5. Discuss how the Israelite community and its leadership change over time.

The texts this week move us between the land of Egypt and the land of promise, between the covenant of Yahweh and the struggles of Israel to stay true to that covenant. God's providence is never in doubt. God's presence is never in question. God's promise is never withdrawn. As a total group, recall the content of Deuteronomy 5–6 and hear Deuteronomy 6:4-25 read aloud. What are the people of Israel called to remember (or "not forget") and why?

Examining God's Word in Context

(15–20 minutes)

Knowing the context of the culture in which the law codes in the Book of Exodus were written, we can read the text with more understanding.

Viewing the Video: Session 3, Part 2

Prepare to View Video:
Listen for archaeological evidence related to the story of the Exodus from Egypt and the Ten Commandments.

After Viewing Video:

While the presentation, on its own, may prompt sufficient discussion by the group, consider one or more of the following approaches to guide the group's response to the information in the video segment.

❖ **Making Connections:** Follow the route of the Exodus on a map. Recall the various stages the people of Israel went through from Egypt to Sinai: making bricks (bondage), crossing the Red Sea (deliverance), wandering in the wilderness (trust, discipline, waiting), and receiving the Law at Mount Sinai (obedience). How do the stages of Israel's story relate to our own pilgrimage of faith?

❖ **Digging Deeper:** Hear what group members learned from reading articles about or descriptions of the following items in a Bible dictionary: Hyksos Dynasty, Ramses II, Hammurabi's Code, and Mount Sinai. How does this information inform our understanding of the story?

❖ **Looking Further:** Have available a copy of the text of Hammurabi's Code (in addition to the printed versions available, several Web sites provide the complete text in English). Show a printed copy to group members, allowing each person to read aloud one of the codes listed. Talk about the similarities between Hammurabi's Code and the Old Testament laws and the purpose and need for such laws in a covenant community.

Going Forth With God's Word: An Invitation to Discipleship

(10–15 minutes)

The texts call to mind God's mighty acts of deliverance and command for obedience, as well as God's call for response from those God has chosen and delivered. Form pairs to discuss the following: What type of bondage exists for the people of God today? How can Christians participate in God's ongoing work of liberation in our world today?

Conclude discussion by calling attention to the "For Reflection" section on page 49 in the participant book. Ask pairs to share responses to one or more of the questions in that section.

Closing and Prayer

Turn to Session 4 and preview the focus of the lesson and the assignments for the week ahead. Be sure to alert group members to the information in the "Digging Deeper" box on page 62 of the participant book.

Promise and Problem in the Land

Gathering Around God's Word

(15–20 minutes)

Welcome
Begin on time by welcoming the group to the study.

Invitation to the Table (Optional)
- **Opening question:** What images come to mind when you think of war?
- **Items for the table:** photographs of war or battle scenes, swords, map of Canaan, pictures of pagan idols, strands of crimson cord

Prayer
- Psalm 119:25-32

Invitation From Scripture
Choose this day whom you will serve, whether the gods your ancestors served in the region beyond the River or the gods of the Amorites in whose land you are living; but as for me and my household, we will serve the LORD. —Joshua 24:15

Viewing the Video: Session 4, Part 1

Prepare to View Video:
Listen for the concept of *herem* and the role it played in the conquest narratives in the Old Testament.

Summary of Video Content:
Ending their wandering in the wilderness and beginning their occupation of the land, Joshua leads the Israelites to conquer the land of Canaan. The first city Israel conquers is Jericho. The city and all that is in it is devoted (*herem*) to the Lord for destruction.

Herem means sparing no life, and anything found in the city—at least anything of value—is likewise "devoted" to God. Any Israelite who does not obey risks bringing harm not only to himself but also to everyone else.

Herem is not a practice unique to the Israelites in the Old Testament. In the ancient context, *herem* was a political given: wars were fought in dedication to the glorification of a national deity, which means everyone and everything taken in battle is "devoted" to that god. *Herem* was part of the ancient landscape.

The focus is not on Israel's political advancement at all costs, but on God. It is God who is behaving in this way. It doesn't matter whether it's against Israel or the Canaanites. The purpose of *herem* was not simply to kill for the sake of killing. Rather, it served as an announcement, both to Israel and her neighbors, that Yahweh is mightier than other gods are.

Discuss After Viewing Video:

What do the conquest narratives bring to the story of God's chosen people? How does the image of God depicted in Joshua compare to the image of God depicted in the stories of Genesis and Exodus? What would be missing from our understanding of Israel's story without the account in Joshua?

Encountering God's Word in the Text

(20–25 minutes)

Our readings this week cover the Israelites' entry into Canaan and the change from a tribal system to a monarchy. Form two groups, one group to focus on the assigned Scriptures from Joshua and Judges, and the other group to focus on the assigned Scriptures from First Samuel. Have the two groups recall the texts and consult any notes made during the week's study to characterize (1) the promise in the land and (2) the problem in the land. How did the people of Israel respond to the promise, and how did they address the problem?

Hear Judges 6:1-18 read aloud. What are we to make of Gideon's response to God's call and his desire for a sign, not once but many times? What is the message of this story for Israel? For us today?

Examining God's Word in Context

(15–20 minutes)

Archaeological evidence points out that the Israelites were living very much like their Canaanite neighbors. However, the difference with the Israelites is they have a dream.

Viewing the Video: Session 4, Part 2

Prepare to View Video:
Listen for archaeological evidence that points to the people of Israel's presence in Canaan.

After Viewing Video:
While the presentation, on its own, may prompt sufficient discussion by the group, consider one or more of the following approaches to guide the group's response to the information in the video segment.

❖ **Making Connections:** Ask persons to share what they know or have learned about the Canaanite religious beliefs and practices. How did having a dream of a Promised Land and the story of a covenant-making God affect the lives of the Israelites? How did it place them at odds with their Canaanite neighbors?

❖ **Digging Deeper:** Hear what group members learned from reading articles about some of the cities mentioned in the conquest narratives of Joshua—Jericho, Ai, Bethel, Hazor—and about the Philistines and their way of life.

❖ **Looking Further:** Using a map of Canaan during the time of Joshua's campaign, follow the path of conquest in the readings for the week. Or, have available a resource containing the text of the Ras Shamra tablets (see *Ancient Near Eastern Texts Relating to the Old Testament*, Volume I, edited by James B. Pritchard, pp.129–155); or a brief article on the Ras Shamra tablets (see *Understanding the Old Testament*, Anderson, pp. 169–171). Compare and contrast Canaanite religious practices with those of early Israel.

Going Forth With God's Word: An Invitation to Discipleship

(10–15 minutes)

What God asks the Israelites to do is trust in God's faithful care in spite of all appearances to the contrary. Talk in pairs about how the world we live in today compares to the world the Israelites encountered in Canaan. What are the gods that we find are hard to leave behind? Why is it so difficult for us to choose every day to serve the God who chose us?

Conclude discussion by calling attention to the "For Reflection" section on page 61 in the participant book. Ask pairs to share responses to one or more of the questions in that section.

Closing and Prayer

Turn to Session 5 and preview the focus of the lesson and the assignments for the week ahead. Be sure to alert group members to the information in the "Digging Deeper" box on page 73 of the participant book.

Israel Has a King

Gathering Around God's Word

(15–20 minutes)

Welcome

Begin on time by welcoming the group to the study.

Invitation to the Table (Optional)
- **Opening question:** What kind of promises did you make as a child? What kind of promises do you make as an adult?
- **Items for the table:** crown, sword, jar of anointing oil, art image of David as king, purple cloth

Prayer
- **Psalm 111**

Invitation From Scripture

Your house and your kingdom shall be made sure forever before me; your throne shall be established forever. —2 Samuel 7:16

Viewing the Video: Session 5, Part 1

Prepare to View Video:

Listen for insights into covenant and how God is faithful even when Israel fails.

Summary of Video Content:

Covenant describes the nature of the relationship between God and humanity. It is a contract of sorts between God and us. The very existence of God's covenant with Israel is God's doing alone. This is why Israel is called the chosen people.

The main features of covenant in the Old Testament are seen through four figures: Noah, Abraham, Moses, and David. *Covenant* is more or less a promise made by God to Noah, his descendants, and all living creatures. The sign of that covenant, of course, is the rainbow. Maybe this was a renewing of the original covenant between God and all of creation— a relationship disrupted by sin.

Abraham is the beginning of what will become Israel, the chosen people. The sign of this covenant is circumcision, signifying Israel's commitment to God.

— Keeping the Law

Moses receives the Law on Mount Sinai. The Law is not a condition to becoming God's people. The Law is what God gives as a means of making Israel into the kind of people God would use to redeem all peoples.

The final major covenant in the Old Testament is with David. But, as the story goes, Israel was not faithful to the covenant. God is always faithful. This is the heart of the biblical idea of covenant.

Discuss After Viewing Video:

The video suggests that the various expressions of covenant in the Old Testament may be seen as a renewal of God's original covenant with all of creation. How does that idea inform our understanding of covenant? Of God? Of Israel? What does it mean to say that the Law was not given as a *condition* to becoming God's people, but as a means for redeeming all people?

Encountering God's Word in the Text

(20–25 minutes)

The material in Second Samuel is a complex portrait of a public figure and a private individual who is finally human, like us. Form two groups. Assign Group 1: 2 Samuel 6–7 and Psalm 89. Assign Group 2: 2 Samuel 11–12 and Psalm 51. Instruct the two groups to follow this procedure:

(1) recall the story in the passage;

(2) summarize the message of the psalm and identify its connection to the story; and

(3) list the character traits of David based on his portrayal in the narrative and through the psalm.

Allow groups to come together to compare portraits of David. Then, ask each group to discuss this question: How does the character of David reflect the character of Israel? **?**

Hear Psalm 18:1-30 read aloud. Ask group members to imagine themselves living in exile in a foreign, hostile country, listening to this psalm. What message would you hear?

Examining God's Word in Context

(15–20 minutes)

David forged Israel into a nation, extending its borders to its furthest reaches, driving out the Philistines. He set up a capital city and brought the ark of the covenant there. Israel was at last a united kingdom with worship consolidated in Jerusalem.

Viewing the Video: Session 5, Part 2

Prepare to View Video:
Listen for references to David, the city of David, and the house of David.

After Viewing Video:
While the presentation, on its own, may prompt sufficient discussion by the group, consider one or more of the following approaches to guide the group's response to the information in the video segment.

❖ **Making Connections:** The Davidic Covenant, stated in 2 Samuel 7, contains an extended play on the word translated in English as *house*. The passage says that the "house of David" would be established forever. Make use of the notes on the passage and on the word play in your study Bible. How does the play on the word *house* give meaning to God's promise for David and for the Israelites?

❖ **Digging Deeper:** Hear what group members learned from reading articles about or descriptions of the following items in a Bible dictionary: Jebusites, Jerusalem, Kidron, and Gihon.

❖ **Looking Further:** On a map of Jerusalem (see *Oxford Bible Atlas*, p. 80), locate the following places: the Dome of the Rock (where the Temple once stood), the city of David, the Kidron Valley and the

Gihon Spring. On a map of Israel and the Ancient Near East (see *Oxford Bible Atlas*, pp. 65, 71, and 75), note the country conquered during King David's reign. Then compare the size of the United Kingdom of Israel with the size of the kingdoms of Assyria, Babylon, and Egypt.

Going Forth With God's Word: An Invitation to Discipleship

(10–15 minutes)

As we read Second Samuel, we are invited to read our own lives and motivations in new ways. We see that the text dares to tell the truth about David. We are challenged to tell the truth about ourselves. In pairs, discuss this question: Where is the Christian community today at risk of desiring to be "like other nations"?

Conclude discussion by calling attention to the "For Reflection" section on page 72 in the participant book. Ask pairs to share responses to the questions in that section.

Closing and Prayer

Turn to Session 6 and preview the focus of the lesson and the assignments for the week ahead. Be sure to alert group members to the information in the "Digging Deeper" box on page 85 of the participant book.

Division and the Rise of Prophecy

Gathering Around God's Word

(15–20 minutes)

Welcome
Begin on time by welcoming the group to the study.

Invitation to the Table (Optional)
- **Opening question:** When was the last time you received a word that contained good news and bad news? How did you respond to the news?
- **Items for the table:** lighted candle, jar of meal, plumb line, grapes, images of objects that keep us from being faithful to God

Prayer
- **Psalm 82**

Invitation From Scripture
What does the LORD require of you / but to do justice, and to love kindness, / and to walk humbly with your God? —Micah 6:8

Viewing the Video: Session 6, Part 1

Prepare to View Video:
Listen for information related to prophets and the prophetic word.

Summary of Video Content:
Three great institutions were active during Israel's monarchic period: prophet, priest, and king. The role of Israel's prophets was significant. An Old Testament prophet is someone called by God to speak God's word to the people. The content of that divine message is very often a challenging, corrective, and even condemning one, not only to the nations around Israel but to Israel as well.

Isaiah, Jeremiah, Ezekiel, and Daniel are "major" prophets mainly because of the length of these books. They are also called "writing" prophets since they have books named after them. Another helpful way of categorizing Israel's prophets is to see them as either "central" or "peripheral" to society. The central prophets were those close to the power centers, be they royal or priestly, who were generally expected to support the official policy (Isaiah, Jeremiah, Ezekiel, Hosea, Amos). Peripheral prophets functioned more on the periphery of the power structures and were free to be more critical of the ruler (Ezekiel, Joel, and Jonah). Whether central or peripheral, Israel's prophets were fundamentally concerned to speak God's word to the king and his people, regardless of how unpopular that word might be.

For Christians today, the prophetic word is to be understood in the context of the church—in its call to live out a life of covenant obedience in the world around us. Because we are in Christ, the prophetic call for justice, righteousness, and faithful obedience to God is still one to be heard—and heeded.

Discuss After Viewing Video:

Discuss the difference between "central" and "peripheral" prophets. The content of the divine message of the Old Testament prophet is often challenging, corrective, and even condemning. How was this message often received by Israel, and what was the people's response? What did the prophetic word say about God's covenant with Israel?

Encountering God's Word in the Text

(20–25 minutes)

This week's readings chronicle the dissolution of David's kingdom and, in particular, the tensions that arise during Solomon's reign. Assign each of three groups one of the following three passages about Solomon: 1 Kings 3:3-15; 1 Kings 5:1-18; and 1 Kings 11:1-13. Have the groups use the following questions to guide their discussion of the passages:

- What tension is revealed in this part of Solomon's story?
- What message is the writer of First Kings trying to send to Israel in this part of Solomon's story?

As the kingdom declines, prophets like Elijah come to prominence, calling attention to a different set of tensions in the land: tensions between Baal and Yahweh, between complacency and justice, and between piety and true religion. This time assign the same three groups a passage featuring Elijah: 1 Kings 17:8-16; 1 Kings 18:17-40; and 1 Kings 21:1-29. In each episode, what message is the writer sending Israel?

(**Optional activity**) Present the prophetic word creatively. Form a new set of three groups to paraphrase the prophetic message in these three passages: Amos 3; Hosea 1–3; and Micah 3. Discuss the prophetic word or words given in the texts. Then prepare some creative way to communicate the message to the total group (for example: write a lyric to a familiar tune, design a billboard or a magazine ad, script a commercial, sketch a banner, use hieroglyphics).

Examining God's Word in Context

(15–20 minutes)

By the end of the eighth century B.C., Israel is essentially part of the Assyrian Empire. The prophets give hope by calling the people to turn to God so they will be spared to dream again.

Viewing the Video: Session 6, Part 2

Prepare to View Video:
Listen for the archaeological evidence that points to the idolatry of the Israelites and the invasion and takeover by other nations.

After Viewing Video:
While the presentation, on its own, may prompt sufficient discussion by the group, consider one or more of the following approaches to guide the group's response to the information in the video segment.

❖ **Making Connections:** Put yourself in the place of the people of Israel. They follow the Lord; yet when the drought comes, they see a need to worship other gods in order to be sure their bases are covered. They hear of and witness the power of the Assyrian army and begin to wonder about the Assyrian gods. Why does power and security have so much influence on the rulers in the land of Israel? It seems throughout Israel's history, as the ruler goes, so goes the people. Why does the ruler's faithfulness carry so much weight among the people?

❖ **Digging Deeper:** Hear what group members learned from reading articles about or descriptions of the following items in a Bible dictionary: Assyrians, Solomon's Temple, high places, Shalmaneser III, Jehu, Sennacharib, Lachish, and Hezekiah.

❖ **Looking Further:** On a map of Israel at the time of Solomon's death, identify the location of the twelve tribes. Locate Jerusalem in the south and Dan in the north. Point out the following places: Negeb Desert, and Lachish.

Going Forth With God's Word: An Invitation to Discipleship

(10–15 minutes)

On his deathbed, David counseled his son Solomon: "Be strong . . . walk before God in faithfulness." Solomon finally opted for the politics of power rather than the wisdom of the heart. In pairs, share with each other the barriers you encounter when walking before God in faithfulness. How does the culture we live in affect your walk in faithfulness? What measures do you need to take "to do justice, to love kindness, and to walk humbly with your God"?

Conclude discussion by calling attention to the "For Reflection" section on page 84 in the participant book. Ask pairs to share responses to one or more of the questions in that section.

Closing and Prayer

Turn to Session 7 and preview the focus of the lesson and the assignments for the week ahead. Be sure to alert the group to the information in the "Digging Deeper" box on page 98 of the participant book.

Exile and Response

Gathering Around God's Word

(15–20 minutes)

Welcome
Begin on time by welcoming the group to the study.

Invitation to the Table (Optional)
- **Opening question:** What comes to mind when you hear the word *exile*?
- **Items for the table:** symbols of Jewish identity (scroll, menorah, Hebrew Bible), shards of broken pottery, bones, unlit candle

Prayer
- **Psalm 137:1-6**

Invitation From Scripture
How could we sing the LORD's song / in a foreign land? —Psalm 137:4

Viewing the Video: Session 7, Part 1

Prepare to View Video:
Listen for ways the Jewish people sought to redefine themselves following the Babylonian destruction of Jerusalem in 586 B.C.

Summary of Video Content:
Traumatic events can shatter our world and force us to redefine ourselves, both as individuals and as communities. The Babylonian destruction of Jerusalem in 586 B.C. and the subsequent exile of thousands of Judeans to Babylon left its mark on the Bible and on the Jewish people.

Those who were settled in Babylon solidified Jewish identity by granting new importance to distinguishing practices such as circumcision, sabbath, and dietary restrictions. The Exile also may have encouraged the beginning stages of the writing of documents that would later be accepted as the Bible.

Many exiled Jews stayed in Babylon, remaining a thriving Jewish community into the twentieth century. The Babylonian Talmud, a core document for Jewish life and practice, was put together by Jews in Babylon. Some Jews had never left the land of Israel. In fact, evidence suggests that modified worship may have continued on the site of the burned Temple.

The books of Ezra and Nehemiah record some of the conflict between the *golah* (those who returned from exile) and "the people of the land" (those who had not been exiled). The books of Ruth and Jonah also may reflect some of these tensions over who belongs within the community and who does not. Forging identity often leads to separation from others. Late biblical books reflect a diversity of views, and by the time of Jesus various understandings of Judaism coexisted, including different understandings of just what it meant to be a Jew.

Discuss After Viewing Video:

Discuss the elements that kept the Jewish people together after their return from exile. Discuss the elements that brought diversity. What challenges did diversity pose for the returning Jews' attempts to remain faithful to God?

Encountering God's Word in the Text

(20–25 minutes)

The Exile, or Babylonian Captivity, forced a realignment of Israel's understanding of who they were and who God would be for them. In their oracles to the exiles, Jeremiah and Ezekiel proclaimed that a new vision was taking shape in the heart of God. In groups of three or four, discuss this new vision and how it would affect the people of God. Have each person in the group identify and share a passage in the readings from Jeremiah and Ezekiel that best illustrates this new vision.

Then as a total group, talk about the issues facing the Jews of the exilic and postexilic eras as they focused on their distinctive identity. Ask group members to use the stories of Esther, Ruth, and Jonah as context to discuss how the Jews are to live in the midst of strangers in a hostile world. How does the message of Esther, Ruth, and Jonah translate into our day?

Examining God's Word in Context

(15–20 minutes)

How Yahweh will dwell with the Jews, and how the Jews will dwell in this often hostile world, are the focal issues of this session's readings.

Viewing the Video: Session 7, Part 2

Prepare to View Video:
Listen for archaeological evidence related to the Babylonian and Persian Empires. Listen also for the difference in how the Hebrew Bible and the Old Testament end.

After Viewing Video:
While the presentation, on its own, may prompt sufficient discussion by the group, consider one or more of the following approaches to guide the group's response to the information in the video segment.

❖ **Making Connections:** Locate the English translation of the text of the Cyrus Cylinder (available online) and read aloud a portion. Then read Cyrus's edict of liberation as recorded in Ezra 1:2-4. Imagine being one of the Jews living in exile and receiving the news of Cyrus's benevolence. How would you respond?

❖ **Digging Deeper:** Hear what group members learned from reading articles about or descriptions of the following items in a Bible dictionary: Nineveh, Nebuchadnezzar, Babylonian Captivity, Cyrus the Great, Persia, and the Diaspora.

❖ **Looking Further:** Take a moment to compare the ending verses of the Old Testament (in Christian Bibles) in Malachi (4:4-6) with the ending verses of the Hebrew Bible (in the TANAKH) in Second Chronicles (36:22-23). Discuss the seed of hope in each and the context from which the words are spoken.

Going Forth With God's Word: An Invitation to Discipleship

(10–15 minutes)

God's purpose for God's chosen people, while special, is not necessarily exclusive. For God is always and everywhere doing a new thing. In pairs, have persons share responses to these questions: Where do you see yourself in your pilgrimage of faith—In exile? At home? In the midst of strangers? What image characterizes your view of God's vision for God's people? Who are we being called to include in that vision today?

Conclude discussion by calling attention to the "For Reflection" section on page 97 in the participant book. Ask pairs to share responses to one or more of the questions in that section.

Closing and Prayer

Turn to Session 8 and preview the focus of the lesson and the assignments for the week ahead. Be sure to alert the group to the information in the "Digging Deeper" box on page 108 of the participant book.

Restoration and Renewal

Gathering Around God's Word

(15–20 minutes)

Welcome
Begin on time by welcoming the group to the study.

Invitation to the Table (Optional)
- **Opening question:** When you think of "the end of time," what image comes to mind?
- **Items for the table:** a variety of lighted candles set on squares of mirrored glass

Prayer
- Psalm 96

Invitation From Scripture
For I am about to create new heavens and a new earth; the former things shall not be remembered or come to mind. —Isaiah 65:17

Viewing the Video: Session 8, Part 1

Prepare to View Video:
Listen for insights into the books of Proverbs, Job, and Ecclesiastes, part of the Wisdom Literature of the Hebrew Bible. **Note:** *Because the subject of the Bible's wisdom books is not covered in the commentary section of the participant book, the subject of this video segment is designed to provide an overview. As a consequence, unlike the other Part 1 video segments, this segment does not deal with themes arising from the assigned Scripture readings for Days 1–5.*

Summary of Video Content:
In the Hebrew Bible, the books of Proverbs, Job, and Ecclesiastes make up most of what is called Wisdom Literature. Proverbs speaks with a

didactic, instructional tone. The voices of Job and Ecclesiastes sound more philosophical. "The fear of the LORD is the beginning of knowledge" is the theme of the Book of Proverbs. What follows is a collection of short, easy-to-remember teachings.

Characteristically, traditional wisdom divides humanity into two groups: the wise (or righteous) and the foolish (or wicked). The fruits of the wise and righteous life are success, well-being, and longevity. The fool, on the other hand, always comes to ruin.

Job and Ecclesiastes take the form of long discourses (Job) and autobiographical reflections (Ecclesiastes) rather than short sayings. The Book of Job is an epic tale, a tale of a man declared righteous by God who nevertheless becomes the victim of unspeakable calamities. Theological reflection on the issue of retribution continues in the Book of Ecclesiastes.

What we have in the Bible's Wisdom Literature is conversation: a conversation among a variety of perspectives, encouraging us to be honest with each other and with God, to be bold in upright living, and to trust God with what we know and with what we cannot know.

Discuss After Viewing Video:
What is knowledge? What is wisdom? What are the characteristics of wisdom literature? How did the Old Testament's Wisdom Literature function as "a conversation among a variety of perspectives" for Israel? How does it function for readers today?

Encountering God's Word in the Text

(20–25 minutes)

The Hebrew Bible closes with three different visions for the future: a heavenly/apocalyptic victory (Daniel); an earthly/political restoration (Ezra/Nehemiah); and a universal/global mission (Second Isaiah). Form three groups and have them review a portion of the daily readings as follows: Group 1: Review the Scriptures for Day 5 and prepare a paragraph describing the apocalyptic vision for the future. Group 2: Review the Scriptures for Days 3 and 4 and prepare a paragraph describing the political restoration vision for the future. Group 3: Review the Scriptures for Days 1 and 2 and prepare a paragraph describing the "light to the nations" vision for the future. Allow time for groups to share their paragraphs with the total group.

Then ask: What role does God play in each of these visions for the future? What role do God's people play in each of these visions for the future?

Examining God's Word in Context

(15–20 minutes)

The Dead Sea Scrolls provide us with a link to a kind of Judaism from which early Christianity arises.

Viewing the Video: Session 8, Part 2

Prepare to View Video:
Listen for information that has been obtained from the Dead Sea Scrolls and how it prepares us to understand Judaism as the faith from which Christianity rises.

After Viewing Video:
While the presentation, on its own, may prompt sufficient discussion by the group, consider one or more of the following approaches to guide the group's response to the information in the video segment.

❖ **Making Connections:** What were some of the findings related to the community of the Qumran community? How do these findings inform our understanding of Judaism and early Christianity as well as the faith traditions of Christians today?

❖ **Digging Deeper:** Hear what group members learned from reading about the following items in a Bible dictionary: Qumran, Dead Sea Scrolls, Messiah, and Jewish funeral practices.

❖ **Looking Further:** Share with group members photographs of the Dead Sea Scrolls. Read segments from the Community Rule that tell why the Qumran community decided to live in the desert. Read segments from the War Scroll, especially the sections referring to the "children of light and the children of darkness." (See *The Complete World of the Dead Sea Scrolls,* by Philip R. Davies, George J. Brooke, and Phillip R. Callaway, for views of the actual scrolls; and see *The Complete Dead Sea Scrolls in English* by Geza Vermes to read the texts.)

Going Forth With God's Word: An Invitation to Discipleship

(10–15 minutes)

The Hebrew Bible or the Old Testament is a story about God from beginning to end: God's blessing of Creation, God's promise to Abraham, God's deliverance of the Hebrews, God's giving of the Law, God's faithfulness in spite of the people's faithlessness, and God's vision of restoration. The invitation to us is to help God finish the story. Form pairs to answer the following question: What actions and/or attitudes are called for to help finish God's story?

Conclude discussion by calling attention to the "For Reflection" section on page 107 in the participant book. Ask pairs to share responses to the questions at the end of that section.

Closing and Prayer

Take time to thank group members for their participation during the study, and lead them in a time of reflection and prayer. Consider allowing persons an opportunity to give thanks for their experiences of learning and fellowship during the course. Then, as a way to celebrate one of the central declarations of the Hebrew Bible, ask the group members to locate Deuteronomy 6:4-6 (the Shema) in their Bibles. (It will help if everyone can read out of the same translation). Then stand and recite together that passage.